REPORT DOCUMENTATION PAGE

1. AGENCY USE ONLY (Leave blank)	2. REPORT DATE September 2007	3. REPORT TYPE AND DATES COVERED Final Report September 2007

4. TITLE AND SUBTITLE

Keys to Efficient Development of Useful Environmental Documents

5. FUNDING NUMBERS

TPA2/EV869

6. AUTHOR(S)

Carl Bausch

7. PERFORMING ORGANIZATION NAME(S) AND ADDRESS(ES)

U.S. Department of Transportation
Research and Innovative Technology Administration
John A. Volpe National Transportation Systems Center
55 Broadway
Cambridge, MA 02142-1093

8. PERFORMING ORGANIZATION REPORT NUMBER

DOT-VNTSC-FTA-07-03

9. SPONSORING/MONITORING AGENCY NAME(S) AND ADDRESS(ES)

Federal Transit Administration
1200 New Jersey Avenue, SE
4th Floor–East Building
Washington, D.C. 20590

10. SPONSORING/MONITORING AGENCY REPORT NUMBER

FTA-MA-26-1023-2007.1

11. SUPPLEMENTARY NOTES

12a. DISTRIBUTION/AVAILABILITY STATEMENT

This document is also available to the public through the National Technical Information Service, Springfield, Virginia 22161.

12b. DISTRIBUTION CODE

13. ABSTRACT (Maximum 200 words)

National Environmental Policy Act (NEPA) documents—environmental impact statements and assessments—inform agency decisionmaking and let the public know about anticipated effects of a proposed Federal action. The fundamental purposes and principles of efficient, effective Federal impact statement preparation are set forth in the Council on Environmental Quality's implementing regulations and guidance that have been in existence for nearly three decades. These implementing regulations stress the need for environmental documents to focus on considerations that are truly useful to decisionmakers and the public.

Over the years, however, a tendency to create excessively long, opaque, and costly environmental impact statements and assessments has surfaced. Instead of describing in reasonable and comprehensible terms the substance of a proposed project's purpose and need, alternatives considered, and potential environmental impacts, these documents are now often sources of confusion and delay in project approval and implementation.

To facilitate improvement in the clarity, analytical value, and overall quality of environmental documents for transit projects, the Federal Transit Administration is reexamining its guidance on and practices for environmental documentation. This handbook is intended as a tool to assist in achieving compliance, utility, and practicality when preparing environmental documents.

14. SUBJECT TERMS

Environmental impact statements, environmental assessments, environmental planning, Federal regulations, environmental documents, transit projects, compliance, utility, practicality.

15. NUMBER OF PAGES

45

16. PRICE CODE

17. SECURITY CLASSIFICATION OF REPORT Unclassified	18. SECURITY CLASSIFICATION OF THIS PAGE Unclassified	19. SECURITY CLASSIFICATION OF ABSTRACT Unclassified	20. LIMITATION OF ABSTRACT Unlimited

Keys to Efficient Development of Useful Environmental Documents

Table of Contents

Introduction

The fundamental purposes and principles of efficient, effective Federal environmental document preparation, set forth in regulations implementing the National Environmental Policy Act (NEPA) and related guidance, have been in place for nearly three decades.[1] These regulations have established realistic quantitative and qualitative targets for environmental documents. In addition to specifying a standard format of study topics, the regulations also stress the need for environmental documents to focus on important issues, sharply reducing the emphasis on background material and insignificant issues.

Over the years, however, a tendency to create excessively long, opaque, and costly environmental impact statements (EIS) and assessments (EA) has surfaced. Instead of describing in reasonable and comprehensible terms the substance of a proposed project's purpose and need, alternatives considered, and potential environmental impacts, these documents are now often sources of confusion and delay in project approval and implementation.

To facilitate improvement in the clarity, analytical value, and overall quality of environmental documents for transit projects, the Federal Transit Administration (FTA) is reexamining its guidance on and practices for environmental documentation. FTA's efforts are designed to better consider and address three issues:

1. Compliance: Do environmental documents satisfy the content requirements of NEPA-implementing regulations and relevant guidance?

2. Utility: Are environmental documents written to be useful to the public and decision makers?

3. Practicality: Are procedural techniques to reduce paperwork and delay (see 40 CFR § 1500.4 and § 1500.5 appended to this document) being effectively employed?

This handbook is intended as a tool to assist in achieving compliance, utility, and practicality when preparing environmental documents. It provides keys to efficiently develop environmental impact statements, environmental assessments, and categorical exclusions.

The section on environmental impact statements offers five keys and eight steps for successfully preparing useful impact statement documentation. Subsequent sections on environmental assessments and categorical exclusions discuss the background, purpose, and appropriate contents of each.

---

1 In Executive Order 11991, issued on May 24, 1977, the Council on Environmental Quality was directed to issue regulations implementing the procedural provisions of NEPA. The NEPA implementing regulations were to "be designed to make the environmental impact statement process more useful to decision makers and the public; and to reduce paperwork and the accumulation of extraneous background data, in order to emphasize the need to focus on real environmental issues and alternatives. They will require impact statements to be concise, clear, and to the point, and supported by evidence that agencies have made the necessary environmental analyses."

Notes

Environmental Impact Statements

Key 1: Begin early.

Integrated environmental planning

The National Environmental Policy Act (NEPA) implementing regulations direct agencies to "integrate the NEPA process with other planning at the earliest possible time to insure that planning and decisions reflect environmental values, to avoid delays later in the process, and to head off potential conflicts" (40 C.F.R. § 1501.2). For proposals that originate at State and local levels, the NEPA implementing regulations require Federal agencies to "cooperate with State and local agencies to the fullest extent possible to reduce duplication between NEPA and State and local requirements" (40 C.F.R. § 1506.2(b)).[2] According to the Council on Environmental Quality (CEQ), "Early environmental planning assures that all reasonable alternatives are explored and that there is ample time to identify and resolve difficult issues so that agency action is not unduly delayed. In an ideal world, NEPA would be effectively employed in the planning process to avoid environmental degradation and thus the felt need to prepare bloated, unavailing [documents]."[3]

> I would argue that, over time, the benefit of avoiding or resolving problems "upstream" will save many millions of dollars now thrown at paperwork exercises and litigation.
>
> *Testimony of Thomas C. Jensen, Before the Task Force on Improving the National Environmental Policy Act of the House Committee on Resources 12 (Spokane, WA, April 23, 2005)*

---

2 Section 6002(c)(3) of the Safe, Accountable, Flexible, Efficient Transportation Equity Act: A Legacy for Users (SAFETEA-LU) (*codified* at 23 U.S.C. § 139(c)(3)) expands upon the authorization contained in § 102(2)(D) of NEPA by providing that:

> [a]ny project sponsor that is a State or local governmental entity receiving funds under this title or chapter 53 of title 49 for the project shall serve as a joint lead agency... for purposes of preparing any environmental document under the National Environmental Policy Act of 1969 and may prepare any such environmental document required in support of any action or approval ... if the Federal lead agency furnishes guidance in such preparation and independently evaluates such document and the document is approved and adopted.

3 Executive Office of the President, Council on Environmental Quality, "Summary of the Proceedings of a Workshop on NEPA Integration: Effective, Efficient Environmental Compliance in the 1990s," 3 (December 1991).

Notes

Key 2: Use, to the fullest extent possible, materials developed in planning processes.

State and local planning and planning for New Starts and Small Starts

Consistent with Sections 134 and 135 of Title 23 of the United States Code (U.S.C.), as amended by § 6001 of the Safe, Accountable, Flexible, Efficient Transportation Equity Act: A Legacy for Users (SAFETEA-LU) (Pub. L. 109-59, August 10, 2005), metropolitan and Statewide transportation planning must take place in a very public process and involve consideration of and strategies for protection and enhancement of the environment. (See generally 23 C.F.R. Part 450 (72 Fed. Reg. 7224 (2007).) In the process, transportation planners are also expected to cooperate with agencies responsible for land use management, natural resources, and environmental protection, among other areas of consideration. The record of these planning processes, if not a part of the NEPA process itself (see below), can serve as a useful foundation for that process. For example, planning processes can help to establish the need for and purposes of subsequently proposed transit projects, a critical aspect of the NEPA process. At the same time, relevant environmental issues for transit projects may be identified early, before the NEPA process has begun, and potential "roadblocks" may thereby be averted. To qualify for FTA's discretionary funding program for new capital investments (§ 5309 New Starts and Small Starts), candidate projects must have resulted from an alternatives analysis study (also known as major investment study or multimodal corridor analysis), which evaluates several modal and alignment options for addressing mobility needs in a given corridor. Alternatives analysis is intended to provide information to local officials on the benefits, costs, and impacts of alternative transportation investments. Alternatives analysis involves a wide range of stakeholders, as well as the general public, and results in selection of a locally preferred alternative that is adopted by the metropolitan planning organization in its financially constrained metropolitan transportation plan. At local discretion, alternatives analysis may be conducted in the context of the NEPA process. In either case, the record of alternatives analysis will serve as the foundation for establishing, in the context of the NEPA process, the need for and purposes of proposed transit projects, as well as the range of alternatives that must be considered.

In developing a NEPA document for a proposed project by a non-Federal applicant, a Federal agency "may accord substantial weight to the preferences of the applicant and/or sponsor in the siting and design of the project."[4] The results of planning processes, including alternatives analyses, may be summarized in the NEPA document and incorporated by reference into it. There is no need to burden the NEPA document with exhaustive descriptions of those planning processes.

Integrate the requirements of NEPA with other planning and environmental review procedures required by law or by agency practice so that all such procedures run concurrently rather than consecutively.

40 C.F.R. § 1500.2(C)

---

4 Citizens Against Burlington v. Busey, 938 F.2d 190, 197 (D.C. Cir. 1991), *cert. denied,* 502 U.S. 994 (1991).

Notes

Key 3: Use the "scoping" process for its intended purpose and get to the point.

Focus on significant environmental issues.

The NEPA implementing regulations provide for a scoping process, which applies by its terms to the environmental impact statement (EIS) process, although a less formal type of scoping is conducted for the environmental assessment process and for documented categorical exclusions (discussed subsequently in this handbook). NEPA "scoping" (40 C.F.R. § 1501.7) has specific and fairly limited objectives: (a) to identify concerns of the affected public and other agencies; (b) to facilitate an efficient environmental impact statement preparation process, through assembling the cooperating and participating agencies, assigning writing tasks, ascertaining related permits and reviews that should be scheduled concurrently, and setting time or page limits, as appropriate; (c) to identify the significant issues associated with alternatives that will be examined in detail in the document, while simultaneously limiting consideration and development of issues that are not truly significant; and (d) to save time in the overall process by helping to ensure that draft statements adequately address relevant issues, reducing the possibility that new comments will cause a statement to be rewritten or supplemented.

Although all of the objectives listed above contribute to an efficient environmental impact statement process, the objective described in (c) is probably the most helpful insofar as facilitating preparation of a focused, meaningful document is concerned. The question remains, however, "How does one gauge whether or not an impact is 'significant?'" With respect to this question, an illuminating point of view was articulated by Federal Circuit Court Judge Richard Posner in a 1985 opinion, which, for ease of reading, is paraphrased below.

> In determining what constitutes a "significant" impact, one that would prompt preparation of an environmental impact statement, we can get little help either from the NEPA implementing regulations or from precedent. So varied are the federal actions that affect the environment—so varied are the environmental effects of those actions—that the decided cases compose a distinctly disordered array, as shown by Professor Rodgers' illustrative comparison of cases in which environmental impact statements were and were not held to be required. In Rodgers' handbook we read, for example, that an environmental impact statement is required for a government loan to build a golf course and park but not for a mock amphibious assault by a battalion of marines on a state park, or for a train shipment of nerve gas, or for certain exploratory mining operations.[5]

Scoping helps insure that real problems are identified early and properly studied; that issues that are of no concern do not consume time and effort...

Council on Environmental Quality

---

5 River Road Alliance v. Corps of Engineers, 764 F.2d 445, 450 (7th Cir. 1985), *cert. denied,* 475 U.S. 1055 (1985).

It is in the NEPA scoping process that potentially significant environmental impacts—those that give rise to the need to prepare an environmental impact statement—should be identified; impacts that are deemed not to be significant need not be developed extensively in the context of the impact statement, thereby keeping the statement focused on impacts of consequence. The significance of some impacts may be easier to gauge than that of others. For example, there are "thresholds" associated with some impact areas—air quality and noise levels, among others—beyond which unhealthful effects (a "significance" criterion) may be experienced. Courts have endorsed use of thresholds in the environmental process, as long as they are not rigidly applied.

As Judge Posner suggests, it is difficult to determine at what point, if any, along the magnitude-of-effect continuum an impact should be deemed "significant;" this is especially true at the early stage—scoping—of document/issue development. Environmental issues involved in a proposed project under review for which a concrete significance determination cannot be made early in the process require careful, continued consideration.

There is a tendency on the part of some document preparers to address every conceivable area of impact that could be associated with transit projects whether or not the area is involved in the project under study. This practice adds needlessly to the length of the document and tends to confuse readers. If an environmental value—historic properties, for example—is not involved, then there is no need to develop (basically target and explain away) the issue in the context of the document. If fear of litigation is a motivating factor in addressing non-issues, then a listing of issues "investigated," but found not to be substantially involved can be included somewhere in the administrative record.

Once the scope of the environmental document, including, in the case of environmental impact statements, significant environmental issues to be addressed, is settled, an annotated outline of the document should be prepared and shared with interested agencies and the public. The outline serves at least three worthy purposes, including (1) documenting the results of the scoping process, whether formal or, in the case of environmental assessments, informal; (2) contributing to the transparency of the process; and (3) providing a clear roadmap for concise development of the environmental document.

Preparation of annotated outlines of impact statements or assessments following formal or informal "scoping" is the best means of assuring development of focused, meaningful environmental documents.

Section 102(2)(C)(ii) of NEPA (42 U.S.C. § 4332(2)(C)(ii)) requires that impact statements identify "adverse" environmental effects that cannot be avoided should the proposed action be implemented, but this does not require exhaustive development of every aspect of every negative impact that may be generated by the proposed action; impacts to the quality of the human environment deemed not to be significant, but sufficiently adverse to warrant attention and not otherwise mitigated, may be noted.

Transit projects may also generate environmental benefits; these should be highlighted as well—an impact statement or environmental assessment should draw attention to positive impacts, not just negative impacts.

It is also true that Congress seeks to foster in public transportation law the development and revitalization of public transportation systems that, among other goals, "minimize environmental impacts." This refrain, however, was not intended to be rights-creating language. Moreover, development and revitalization of public transportation systems, including the minimization of environmental impacts, is a shared responsibility among Federal, State, and local governments and the people.

Much can and should be done in the transportation planning process to ensure development of sound, safe, public transportation systems that promote a high-quality environment long before they become "Federalized" for purposes of the NEPA process. The money saved in developing focused environmental documents can go a long way toward the Congressional goal of minimizing any adverse environmental impacts associated with transit projects.

Notes

_____

_____

_____

_____

_____

_____

_____

_____

_____

_____

_____

_____

_____

_____

_____

_____

_____

_____

_____

Key 4: Limit descriptive material that has no bearing on environmental effects (including interrelated social and economic impacts) of consequence, and use plain language in document development.

Write for the layperson and keep the document focused.

Another tendency of document preparers is to burden impact statements and environmental assessments with a considerable amount of extraneous descriptive language. This practice tends to divert readers' attention from environmental impacts of consequence and to confuse issues. Here, again, a well-constructed, annotated outline of the environmental document, composed following the formal or informal scoping process, will help document preparers to remain focused on impacts of consequence and keep extraneous descriptive language to a minimum.

The NEPA implementing regulations require that environmental impact statements "be written in plain language" (40 C.F.R. § 1502.8). The regulations also encourage the use of "appropriate graphics." Agencies are expected to employ writers of clear prose, which is extremely important if documents are going to be meaningful to decisionmakers and the public. Guidance for writing in plain language is available at several websites; two are provided below.

> http://www.plainlanguage.gov/

> http://www.epa.gov/plainlanguage/faqs.htm

It is noteworthy that the NEPA implementing regulations provide that "[e]nvironmental impact statements shall be concise, clear, and to the point, and shall be *supported* by evidence that agencies have made the necessary environmental analyses" (40 C.F.R. § 1500.2(b)) [emphasis supplied]. This means that the impact statement itself does not have to contain elaborate and extensive analyses of different types of impacts but only relatively brief descriptions in plain language of the results of those analyses; the brief descriptions should relate to impacts associated with alternatives that were analyzed and be presented in comparative form to be most helpful to readers. The actual analyses—the material that "supports" the plain language descriptions contained in the impact statement—can be made a part of the administrative record, which can be referenced in the impact statement.

In relating impacts of consequence, document preparers often include highly technical and scientific terminology, such as equations and symbols that the public may not comprehend. Results of technical analyses should be related to the public in understandable terms. For example, document preparers should not explain noise levels in terms of dBA, L_{dn}, and L_{eq}; rather, noise levels should be related in terms of an event with which the public may be familiar, such as standing 10 feet from an idling gasoline-powered lawnmower.

It is important to note methodologies employed in arriving at conclusions involving scientific inquiries. But lengthy discussions of methodologies and technical terminology should be relegated to an appendix of the document.

Acronyms are the language of the bureaucracy and abound in the transit business. But acronyms are like a foreign language to the public; documents that contain a wealth of acronyms discourage readers, who are forced constantly to refer back to glossaries of terms in order to understand the writing. Be kind to readers and avoid excessive use of acronyms in NEPA documents.

Key 5: Control the process.

NEPA and SAFETEA-LU vest considerable authority in the Federal lead agency.

If complexities and nuances of the NEPA process can often challenge environmental law attorneys, imagine how intimidating the process might be for a non-lawyer practitioner, or better yet, a community planner whose NEPA duties are just one of many job-related responsibilities. It is quite easy for someone not well versed in the NEPA process to lose control of that process when confronted with demands, however unreasonable, of so-called NEPA "experts." Or, when threatened with a lawsuit by project opponents or their counsel, the non-expert may very well acquiesce to their wishes, regardless of their merit or lack thereof.

An efficient NEPA process, including document preparation, requires that the responsible Federal official take and maintain control of the process. As more than one court has noted, "The preparation of an environmental impact statement necessarily calls for judgment and that judgment belongs to the agency."[6] The question arises, then, "How well versed in the NEPA process must a 'non-expert' be in order to be able to control the process?" The process will be "controlled" or not at the early stage of development, where the framework of the study is fabricated. By focusing on and becoming familiar with requirements of the early stage of the NEPA environmental impact statement process, the non-expert will be well equipped to control that process. The non-expert, therefore, will need to become familiar with requirements pertaining to scoping, a concept that is defined in the NEPA implementing regulations and has already been treated to a substantial degree.

The NEPA scoping process has been supplemented by provisions of SAFETEA-LU. In determining the proper scope of study, the range of actions, alternatives, and impacts must be considered. Again, a distinction is made between the range of reasonable alternatives to a proposed action advanced by a Federal agency and the range of reasonable alternatives advanced by a non-Federal applicant or sponsor.

Consideration of alternatives is said to be "the heart of the environmental impact statement." All "reasonable" alternatives are to be rigorously explored and objectively evaluated; for alternatives eliminated from detailed study, reasons for doing so must be supplied. There is no hard-and-fast rule regarding what constitutes a reasonable range of alternatives; rather, as the Council on Environmental Quality has observed, "What constitutes a reasonable range of alternatives depends on the nature of the proposal and the facts of each case." At the same time, courts have recognized that "the concept of alternatives must be bounded by some notion of feasibility;" NEPA does not "require detailed discussion of the environmental effects of 'alternatives' put forward in

> **Military environmental law attorneys are often challenged by the complexities and nuances of compliance with provisions of the NEPA process.**
>
> Tozzi, *Mitigation Measures in Analyses under the National Environmental Policy Act*, Army Lawyer (Sept. 2002)

---

6 City of Angoon v. Hodel, 803, F.2d 1016, 1021 (9th Cir. 1986) (*citing* Lathan v. Brinegar, 506 F.2d 677, 693 (9th Cir. 1974)), *cert. denied* 484 U.S. 870 (1987).

comments when these effects cannot be readily ascertained and the alternatives are deemed only remote and speculative possibilities."[7] The range of alternatives to be considered "need not extend beyond those reasonably related to the purposes of the project."[8]

Agencies have substantial discretion in determining the purposes of and need for a proposed action. Section 139(f)(2) of Title 23 of the U.S.C., added by § 6002(f)(2) of SAFETEA-LU, provides that "the lead agency shall define the project's purpose and need for purposes of any document which the lead agency is responsible for preparing for the project." Once established, a project's stated purpose will guide consideration of alternatives; moreover, as courts have recognized, if "an alternative does not implement the purposes of the project it certainly is not reasonable and no purpose would be served by requiring a detailed discussion of its environmental effects since the alternative will never be adopted."[9]

Where a Federal agency is evaluating the proposal of a non-Federal applicant (a transit agency, for example), a somewhat different purpose and need may guide consideration of alternatives. Although the Federal agency has the responsibility for deciding which alternatives to consider in an environmental impact statement, courts have condoned agency evaluation of alternatives focused by the primary objective of a non-Federal applicant. The Council on Environmental Quality has recognized that an agency's evaluation of alternatives may be focused by the primary objectives of a non-Federal applicant, although agencies also have a responsibility to look beyond a non-Federal applicant's goals.[10]

Purposes a non-Federal applicant may advance for consideration in support of its proposal can or may include achieving economic goals and technological objectives, among others. In developing alternatives for consideration in environmental impact statements, a Federal agency "may accord substantial weight to the preferences of the applicant and/or sponsor in the siting and design of the project." As one court has observed, "Congress did not expect agencies to determine for the applicant what the goals of the applicant's proposal should be."[11]

---

7 Vermont Yankee Nuclear Power Corp. v. Natural Resources Defense Council, 435 U.S. 519, 551 (1978).

8 Trout Unlimited v. Morton, 509 F.2d 1276, 1286 (9th Cir. 1974).

9 See I-35E v. Dole, 583 F.Supp. 653, 659-660 (D. Minn. 1984).

10 Executive Office of the President, Council on Environmental Quality, *Environmental Quality 1986* 236 (17th Annual Report, 1988). ("Taken together, the NEPA case law on this issue requires consideration of both public and private purpose and need. The agency may properly focus its evaluation of alternatives based upon the applicant's goals, but it must also exercise independent judgment regarding the appropriate articulation of the objective's purpose and need and the reasonableness of various alternatives.")

11 Citizens Against Burlington v. Busey, 938 F.2d 190, 199 (D.C. Cir. 1991), *cert. denied*, 502 U.S. 994 (1991).

The Environmental Impact Statement Process, as Supplemented by SAFETEA-LU—Step by Step

Step 1: Project initiation

Providing notice

Project and process initiation begins when FTA is notified by the project sponsor who intends to seek Federal funding regarding "the type of work, termini, length, and general location of the proposed project, together with a statement of any Federal approvals anticipated to be necessary for the proposed project, for the purpose of informing [FTA] that the environmental review process should be initiated" (23 U.S.C. § 139(e)).

Step 2: Beginning the "scoping process"

Early intersection of SAFETEA-LU and NEPA

Here is where the process may tend to get a little confusing and could get drawn out needlessly. Very early in the environmental process, Section 139 of Title 23 of the U.S.C., added by § 6002 of SAFETEA-LU, requires that the lead agency (1) extend an invitation to other Federal and non-Federal agencies that may have an interest in the proposed project to become "participating agencies," (2) provide an opportunity for involvement by participating agencies and the public in defining the NEPA "purpose and need" for the proposed project as well as the range of alternatives for consideration in the impact statement, and (3) establish a plan for coordinating public and agency participation in and comment on the environmental review process (which may be established for a category of projects); such a plan may include a schedule for completion of the environmental review process. Though mandated by Section 139 of Title 23 of the U.S.C., the bulk of these requirements actually form part of the NEPA "scoping process," which need not be duplicated but must be preceded by the lead agency's publication in the *Federal Register* of a "Notice of Intent," defined as a notice that an environmental impact statement will be prepared and considered. The notice shall briefly:

(a) Describe the proposed action and possible alternatives.
(b) Describe the agency's proposed scoping process, including whether, when, and where any scoping meeting will be held.
(c) State the name and address of a person within the agency who can answer questions about the proposed action and the environmental impact statement (40 C.F.R. § 1508.22).

How can the requirements of Section 139 of Title 23 of the U.S.C. best be met without unduly burdening the NEPA process?

In an "ideal" situation, shortly after being notified by a sponsor that the environmental review process should be initiated, the lead agency (FTA and/or the project sponsor) would cause a Notice of Intent to be prepared. Because the Notice of Intent, as described below, involves the public and potential "participating agencies," a coordination plan should be established prior to publication of the Notice of Intent in the *Federal Register*. As acknowledged in guidance implementing § 6002 of SAFETEA-LU, elements of coordination plans may be quite similar for actions within the same class; a coordination plan for a category of actions may very well substantially satisfy the requirement for most coordination plans within that category. To the extent that a particular proposal necessitates modifications of a "category" plan, such modifications may be appended or tiered to the category plan. A sample plan is provided in the appendix to this handbook.

In addition to containing information required to be included in a Notice of Intent, the notice should also *preliminarily* identify the purposes of and need for the proposed project, as well as alternatives that may meet those purposes and need. This notice, then, actually signals the beginning of the NEPA scoping process. The Notice of Intent should include sufficient—but not excessive—background information to enable the public and potential participating agencies to understand (1) the origins of the proposed action (by summarizing in a paragraph the results of previous transportation planning efforts, which may be incorporated by reference); (2) the affected environment; and (3) the potentially significant impacts to the affected environment. It is not necessary that the notice contain a wealth of descriptive material; the notice should provide enough information, which admittedly will vary from case to case, to enable the public and potential participating agencies to understand the nature of the proposal and to participate meaningfully at the outset of the scoping process.

At this point, an opportunity for "involvement" by the public in helping to define or redefine the statement of purpose and need, as well as the alternatives to be considered, is provided. Comment on the notice should be invited; a 30-day comment period should be announced. A sample Notice of Intent is provided in the appendix to this handbook.

The Notice of Intent should be appended to invitations, extended by the lead agency to Federal and non-Federal agencies and Indian tribes that may have an interest in the proposed project, to become "participating agencies." In the notice itself, the identity of potential participating agencies may be provided. In many cases, it may be difficult to identify all Federal and non-Federal agencies and Indian tribes that may have an interest in a proposed project. For this reason, the Notice of Intent should also indicate that any Federal or non-Federal agencies and Indian tribes interested in the proposed project that do not receive an invitation to become a participating agency should notify the lead agency of its interest in the proposed project. Potential participating agencies should be given 30 days to respond to the invitation. A sample invitation to become a participating agency is provided in the appendix to this handbook.

The initial phase of the NEPA scoping process, one that satisfies the early coordination requirements of Section 139 of Title 23 of the U.S.C., could be completed within a couple of months of sponsor notification.

Step 3: Annotated outline

A necessary step to achieve objectives of the NEPA process

In the event that scoping meetings are convened (such meetings could satisfy the requirements of 49 U.S.C. § 5323(b)) or further scoping is conducted by other means, the results should be concisely documented, after which an annotated outline of the impact statement should be prepared and then reviewed and approved by the responsible official for the Federal lead agency. The annotated outline should be structured consistent with the format prescribed in the NEPA implementing regulations at 40 C.F.R. § 1502.10.

In preparing an annotated outline of the impact statement,[12] drafters should take full advantage of the NEPA implementing regulations and related guidance to structure a document that conforms to the goals of the regulations, namely "to make the environmental impact statement process more useful to decisionmakers and the public; and to reduce paperwork and the accumulation of extraneous background data, in order to emphasize the need to focus on real environmental issues and alternatives" by requiring "impact statements to be concise, clear, and to the point, and supported by evidence that agencies have made the necessary environmental analyses." To accomplish these goals, annotated outlines should establish the foundation for documents that will, to the fullest extent possible:

- Focus on significant issues to be treated, not issues that are not significant or have been treated elsewhere, which should be eliminated from detailed study (40 C.F.R. § 1501.7(a)(2) and (3)).

- Be concise (normally less than 150 pages; 40 C.F.R. § 1502.7) by fixing page limits for the impact statement and sections of the impact statement (40 C.F.R. § 1501.7(b)(1)); for example, the statement of purpose and need is to be "brief" (40 C.F.R. § 1502.13)—according to the Council on Environmental Quality, seldom longer than one page.

- Adhere to schedules by establishing (for internal use at least) flexible time limits for the entire NEPA process (40 C.F.R. § 1501.8).

- Limit descriptive passages to only what is necessary to understand the nature of the issues (40 C.F.R. § 1502.15).

To the extent that agencies have built the criteria specified in section 101 into their assumptions and policies and have utilized the planning procedures indicated in section 102(2)(A) and (B), the impact statement need be no more than a summary of agency action. Acknowledging exceptions, it may be generalized that impact statements of great length and detail indicate programs or projects of dubious environmental merit.

Lynton K. Caldwell, Special Assistant to the Senate Committee on Interior and Insular Affairs on the drafting of NEPA

---

12 The same provisions highlighted in the NEPA implementing regulations to reduce paperwork and delay in the preparation of impact statements (40 C.F.R. §§ 1500.4 and 1500.5) apply with equal force to preparation of environmental assessments. A distinction is to be drawn, however, inasmuch as environmental assessments (1) will conclude with findings of no significant impact or mitigated findings of no significant impact and therefore focus on "consequential"—not necessarily "significant"—environmental issues; (2) are "concise public documents," which the Council on Environmental Quality advises should be no more than 10 to 15 pages in length; and (3) include only brief discussions of the need for the proposal of alternatives, as required by section 102(2)(E) of NEPA, of the environmental impacts of the proposed action and alternatives, and a listing of agencies and persons consulted (40 C.F.R. § 1508.9).

- Avoid duplicating discussions in different sections of the impact statement (40 C.F.R. § 1502.16).

- Incorporate material by reference whenever possible (40 C.F.R. § 1502.21).

- Adopt other draft or final impact statements or portions of impact statements, as appropriate (40 C.F.R. § 1506.3).

- Eliminate duplication with State and local agency procedures (40 C.F.R. § 1506.2).

- Be written in plain language, employing appropriate graphics (40 C.F.R. § 1502.8).

Even if the responsible Federal official is unable to exercise a high degree of control over the remaining steps (most of which would be included in a coordination plan), production of a solid annotated outline virtually assures development of an impact statement that meets the goals of the NEPA implementing regulations, thereby reducing costs of document preparation and reducing delays, including those associated with review times and the need to "retrace steps."

FHWA has issued valuable guidance on document preparation, which may be accessed at: http://www.environment.transportation.org/pdf/IQED-1_for_CEE.pdf.

Step 4: Follow-up conferences

Checking in

Following review and approval of the annotated outline by the responsible Federal official, conduct occasional conferences with the sponsor and its consultants to ensure that the annotated outline is being followed.

Step 5: The draft impact statement

Public review

After reviewing and approving the draft impact statement, send the requisite number of copies to Headquarters (Office of Planning and Environment) for submission to the U.S. Environmental Protection Agency; arrange for a date, time, and location for a public hearing on the draft impact statement to be held during the 45-day comment period (if public scoping meetings were not held, this meeting could satisfy the requirements of 49 U.S.C. § 5323(b)); and publish notice of the hearing in a local newspaper of general circulation.

Step 6: Constructing the final impact statement

Responding to public comments

Initiate preparation of the final impact statement, taking into account consequential issues raised in comments on the draft impact statement. Here is another area where taking full advantage of the NEPA implementing regulations can save time and resources. Consider the following:

- Each substantive comment that is deemed to have merit does not necessarily have to be addressed separately. Agencies are required to "assess and consider comments both individually and collectively" (40 C.F.R. § 1503.4(a)) but may combine (through an indexing system, for example) comments that raise similar issues and address them in a single response.

- When there is an "exceptionally voluminous" response, "summaries" of comments received may be attached to the final EIS (40 C.F.R. § 1503.4(b)). It is within the discretion of the agency to determine what constitutes an "exceptionally voluminous" response. Much, of course, will depend on the complexity of issues presented, the number of text pages in the draft and final documents, the number and page length of comments, and other relevant factors. When the page length of original (not "canned") comments approaches 50 percent of the page length of a "normal" (as that term is understood in 40 C.F.R. § 1502.7) impact statement, agencies should consider preparing summaries of comments to be attached to the final document. Where summaries are used, the actual comments should be made available for inspection at a convenient repository.

- In certain circumstances, an "errata sheet" final statement may be issued. This statement may be likened simply to a ratification of the way in which the draft document handled alternatives and predictions. Its use is appropriate where an agency's response to comments on the draft is limited to making factual corrections and/or explaining why comments do not warrant further agency response. Errata sheet final statements comprise comments, responses, and changes, which are all that need be circulated to commenters, except that the entire document with a new cover must be filed with the U.S. Environmental Protection Agency (40 C.F.R. § 1503.4(c)). Several copies of the draft should be kept on hand to be able to accommodate requests for copies of the "final" statement from persons who did not participate at the "draft" stage of the process.

- An agency cannot simply ignore the comments of vocal minorities whose private agendas have virtually nothing to do with the focus of the draft document. No comment—even one lacking any merit whatsoever—should be completely ignored. At the very least, every original comment, whether or not it "is thought to merit individual discussion by the agency in the text of the statement" (40 C.F.R. §

19

1503.4(b)), should be attached to the final statement. Where comments not thought to merit individual discussion have been filed, agencies should include in the final document a statement to the effect that "all other comments have been thoroughly considered but none raises any issue that was not adequately dealt with in the draft statement; accordingly, no further response is necessary."

- Except in cases where comment "summaries" are appropriate, reproductions of comments received on the draft document must be attached to the final EIS. The comments may be reduced—two or more to the printed page—in furtherance of paperwork reduction goals and to save copying and mailing expenses. In the case of "canned comments," hundreds of which may be received for a controversial proposal, only one copy of the comment needs to be included in the document, together with a list of names submitting these comments.

- Comments received after the close of the comment due date should be considered, if at all possible. Simply note that such comments were late-filed but "are treated within, to the extent time permits, consistent with the purposes of NEPA and other essential considerations of national policy," or words to that effect.

Step 7: The final impact statement

Just one more step remaining

After reviewing and approving the final impact statement, send the requisite number of copies to Headquarters (Office of Planning and Environment) for submission to the U.S. Environmental Protection Agency.

Step 8: The record of decision

The conclusion of the NEPA environmental impact statement process

Initiate, review, and approve the record of decision. The NEPA implementing regulations provide a framework around which decisionmakers are expected to build their decisions. Section 1505.2 of the NEPA implementing regulations provides that records of decision contain (1) a statement of what the decision was; (2) the identification of all alternatives considered by the agency, including the environmentally preferable alternative(s); (3) a discussion of all factors—economic, technical, and mission-related, as well as considerations of national policy that were balanced in the decisionmaking process and how each factor weighed in the decision; and (4) an explanation of whether the decision was designed to avoid or minimize environmental harm and, if not, why not. These ingredients can be arranged with appropriate emphasis to suit just about any circumstance. Conditions or mitigation committed to in the record of decision are enforceable; decisionmakers and non-Federal applicants seeking Federal funding should not make promises they do not intend to keep.

Note: It is apparent, in the eight steps identified above, that the most important steps are the first three, which generally take place within two or three months of project initiation. In this regard, one expert has observed: "The [National Environmental Conflict Resolution Advisory] Committee placed particular emphasis on the importance and effectiveness of agency efforts to engage with potentially interested parties very early in the process of setting policy, defining programs, or framing projects. The investment of time, effort, and thought 'upstream' can reduce the risk of disputes 'downstream,' when positions may have hardened and options narrowed."[13]

---

13 See testimony of Thomas C. Jensen, Chairman, National Environmental Conflict Resolution Advisory Committee, U.S. Institute for Environmental Conflict Resolution, Before the Task Force on Improving the National Environmental Policy Act of the House Committee on Resources 11 (Spokane, WA, April 23, 2005), http://www.sonnenschein.com/docs/docs_enviro/NEPA_Task_Force_Test.pdf.

Notes

Environmental Assessments, Categorical Exclusions, and Documented Categorical Exclusions

Environmental Assessments

The environmental assessment process is defined in the NEPA implementing regulations as "a concise public document" containing "brief discussions of the need for the proposal, of alternatives as required by Section 102(2)(E), of the environmental impacts of the proposed action and alternatives, and a listing of agencies and persons consulted" (40 C.F.R. § 1508.9). Section 102(2)(E) of NEPA requires agencies to "study, develop, and describe appropriate alternatives to recommended courses of action in *any* proposal that involves unresolved conflicts concerning alternative uses of available resources" [emphasis supplied]. Consideration of alternatives under Section 102(2)(E) of NEPA has been determined by many courts to constitute "an independent requirement of wider scope than consideration of alternatives under the EIS requirement."

Most courts agree that the "role of the EA is to 'provide sufficient evidence and analysis for determining whether to prepare an environmental impact statement or a finding of no significant impact.'"[14] An environmental assessment can also serve to "aid an agency's compliance with the Act when no environmental impact statement is necessary." Presumably, this relates to Section 102(2)(E) of the Act, compliance with which is not optional.

Insofar as the range of alternatives to be considered in the context of the environmental assessment process is concerned, opinion is sharply divided among the circuits. Some circuits subscribe to the view that "the range of alternatives that reasonably must be considered decreases as the environmental impact of the proposed action becomes less and less."[15] These circuits tend to view the role of the environmental assessment as somewhat more limited. Other circuits take a broader view of the environmental assessment process, relying principally on NEPA's Section 102(2)(E) requirement to consider alternatives, thereby likening it to Section 102(2)(C)(iii)'s mandate. In every case, however, great care should be exercised in defining the "need" for a proposed action; it is on that issue courts must ultimately focus in deciding whether the range of alternatives considered satisfies NEPA's requirements.

---

14 Oregon Natural Resources Council v. Lyng, 882 F.2d 1417, 1422 (9th Cir. 1989).

15 Olmstead Citizens for a Better Community v. U.S., 793 F.2d 201, 208-09 (8th Cir. 1986) ("It is 'something of an anomaly' to require that an agency search for more environmentally sound alternatives to a project which it has determined, through its decision not to file an impact statement, will have no significant environmental effects anyway ... cf. *Hanly v. Kleindienst,* 471 F.2d 823, 837 (2d Cir. 1972) (Friendly, C.J., dissenting) (warning of danger of requiring procedures nearly as burdensome as with impact statement despite insignificance of environmental effects) *cert. denied,* 412 U.S. 908 (1973)).

If a proposed action is not classified as requiring an environmental impact statement or categorically excluded, the NEPA implementing regulations tell the agency to prepare an environmental assessment upon which it must base a determination whether to prepare an environmental impact statement. The effort put forth in environmental assessment preparation will not be lost if an environmental impact statement subsequently has to be prepared. And it still may be possible to forgo preparation of an environmental impact statement, even when the environmental assessment process reveals potential "significance," through adoption of mitigation strategies. While it is generally true that an environmental impact statement must be prepared for any major Federal action significantly affecting the quality of the human environment, courts have determined that "if a mitigation condition eliminates all significant environmental effects, no EIS is required."[16]

Records of decision are not required for the environmental assessment process, only for cases requiring environmental impact statements.

The NEPA implementing regulations provide that, in certain limited circumstances, the agency shall make the finding of no significant impact, which must include the environmental assessment or a summary of it, available for public review (including State and areawide clearinghouses) for 30 days before the agency makes its final determination whether to prepare an environmental impact statement and before the action may begin. The circumstances are that the proposed action is, or is closely similar to, one which normally requires the preparation of an environmental impact statement, or the nature of the proposed action is one without precedent (see 40 C.F.R. § 1501.4(e)). The FTA's environmental procedures (23 C.F.R. § 771.119(h)) provide that "When the Administration expects to issue a FONSI for an action described in Sec. 771.115(a) [describing actions normally requiring preparation an environmental impact statement], copies of the EA shall be made available for public review (including the affected units of government) for a minimum of 30 days before the Administration makes its final decision (See 40 CFR 1501.4(e)(2).) This public availability shall be announced by a notice similar to a public hearing notice."

All other environmental assessments and findings of no significant impact "must be available to the public." According to the Council on Environmental Quality, Section 1506.6 "requires agencies to involve the public in implementing their NEPA procedures, and this includes public involvement in the preparation of EAs and FONSIs. These are public 'environmental documents' under Section 1506.6(b), and, therefore, agencies must give public notice of their availability." The objective "is to notify all interested or affected parties."

While the NEPA implementing regulations do not require agencies to invite comment on environmental assessments (other than the implied invitation in § 1501.4(e)(2)), a few courts have taken a somewhat more liberal view of the process. In one case, the court stated:

_____

16 Roanoke River Basin Ass'n v. Hudson, 940 F.2d 58, 62 (4th Cir. 1991).

> The importance of an EA or an EIS lies not merely in the aid it
> may give to the agency's own decisionmaking process, but
> also in the notice it gives the public of both the environmental
> issues the agency is aware of and those it has missed. The EA
> or EIS should provide a springboard for public comment,
> bringing to the agency viewpoints and options it might
> otherwise lack.[17]

Preparation of environmental assessments for transit projects is governed by §§ 771.119 and 771.121 of the FTA's implementing procedures. Applicants are responsible for preparing, in consultation with the agency, environmental assessments for actions that are not categorically excluded and do not clearly require the preparation of an environmental impact statement, or where the agency believes preparation of an environmental assessment would assist in determining the need for an environmental impact statement. Early consultation and identification of consequential environmental issues and review requirements are encouraged. Environmental assessments, as well as findings of no significant impact, if executed, must be made available to the public with an opportunity for comment.

According to the Council on Environmental Quality, an environmental assessment is "a concise public document," which "should not contain long descriptions or detailed data;" instead, "it should contain a brief discussion of the need for the proposal, alternatives to the proposal, the environmental impacts of the proposed action and alternatives, and a list of agencies and persons consulted."[18] The Council has generally advised agencies to keep the length of environmental assessments to not more than approximately 10 to 15 pages. To avoid undue length, the environmental assessment may incorporate by reference background data to support its concise discussion of the proposal and relevant issues.

Lengthy environmental assessments are discouraged, "except in unusual cases, where a proposal is so complex that a concise document cannot meet the goals of Section 1508.9 and where it is extremely difficult to determine whether the proposal could have significant environmental effects."[19] The Council has found that, in most cases, a lengthy environmental assessment "indicates that an EIS is needed."

In a memorandum dealing with emergency actions and NEPA, the Council on Environmental Quality outlined how agencies should prepare focused, concise, and timely environmental assessments. Although the memorandum relates to emergency situations, the environmental assessment guidance has much broader application.

Read about how agencies should prepare focused, concise, and timely environmental assessments by clicking on the link provided below:
September 8 2005 Memorandum: Emergency Actions and NEPA

---

17 Illinois Commerce Comm'n v. ICC, 848 F.2d 1246, 1260 (D.C. Cir. 1988).

18 Council on Environmental Quality, Forty Most Asked Questions Concerning the Council on Environmental Quality's National Environmental Policy Act Regulations, 46 Fed. Reg. 18026, 18037 (1981) (answer to Question 36a).

19 *Ibid.* (answer to Question 36b).

If an environmental assessment is intended to conclude the NEPA process, the agency must issue a "finding of no significant impact" (often referred to as a FONSI), which means a document "briefly presenting the reasons why an action, not otherwise excluded (§ 1508.4), will not have a significant effect on the human environment and for which an environmental impact statement therefore will not be prepared" (40 C.F.R. § 1508.13). This requirement was included in the NEPA implementing regulations largely as a response to early court decisions holding that agencies must prepare a reviewable record relative to the question of whether an environmental impact statement is required. The finding itself need not be detailed but must succinctly state the reasons for deciding that the action will have no significant environmental effects and, if relevant, must show which factors were weighted most heavily in the determination. In addition to this statement, the finding must include, summarize, or attach and incorporate by reference the environmental assessment.

In preparing environmental assessments, the same principles that apply to efficient, effective preparation of impact statements—making the document useful to decisionmakers by focusing concisely and clearly only on issues pertinent to the question of environmental "significance," and providing support for the ultimate determination—apply to environmental assessments.

Categorical Exclusions and Documented Categorical Exclusions

Many actions may qualify as categorically excluded from the need to prepare either an environmental impact statement or an environmental assessment. Categorical exclusions are defined in the FTA implementing procedures as "actions which meet the definition contained in 40 CFR 1508.4, and, based on past experience with similar actions, do not involve significant environmental impacts. They are actions which: do not induce significant impacts to planned growth or land use for the area; do not require the relocation of significant numbers of people; do not have a significant impact on any natural, cultural, recreational, historic or other resource; do not involve significant air, noise, or water quality impacts; do not have significant impacts on travel patterns; or do not otherwise, either individually or cumulatively, have any significant environmental impacts" (23 C.F.R. § 771.117(a)). Actions that normally would be classified as categorically excluded but could involve extraordinary circumstances may require preparation of appropriate environmental studies to determine if the categorical exclusion is proper. Such unusual circumstances include (1) significant environmental impacts; (2) substantial controversy on environmental grounds; (3) significant impact on properties protected by Section 4(f) of the Department of Transportation Act or Section 106 of the National Historic Preservation Act; or (4) inconsistencies with any Federal, State, or local law, requirement or administrative determination relating to the environmental aspects of the action (23 C.F.R. § 771.117(b)).

A total of 20 types of action have been determined to meet the criteria of § 771.117(a); a link to the listing of those actions is provided below:

> http://a257.g.akamaitech.net/7/257/2422/10apr20061500/edocket.access.gpo.gov/cfr_2006/aprqtr/23cfr771.117.htm

The Council on Environmental Quality believes that sufficient information will usually be available during the course of normal project development to determine the need for an impact statement and that the agency's administrative record will clearly document the basis for its decision. Accordingly, the Council has strongly discouraged procedures that would require the preparation of additional paperwork to document that an activity has been categorically excluded. Courts, on the other hand, have held that it is "difficult to determine if the application of an exclusion is arbitrary and capricious where there is no contemporaneous documentation to show that the agency considered the environmental consequences of its action and decided to apply a categorical exclusion to the facts of a particular decision. Post hoc invocation of a categorical exclusion does not provide assurance that the agency actually considered the environmental effects of its action before the decision was made."[20] Accordingly, a brief written statement demonstrating that the agency considered the environmental consequences of its action and decided to apply a categorical exclusion to the facts of the case should be included in the administrative record. For actions listed in § 771.117(c), the information developed in Transportation Electronic Award and Management system serves this function.

Section 771.117(d) of the implementing procedures provides examples of actions that may be determined to be categorically excluded only after Administration approval. Applicants must submit documentation that demonstrates that the specific conditions or criteria for the categorical exclusions are satisfied and that significant environmental effects will not result. Examples of such actions may be viewed by clicking on the link below:

> http://a257.g.akamaitech.net/7/257/2422/10apr20061500/edocket.acces
> s.gpo.gov/cfr_2006/aprqtr/23cfr771.117.htm

In documenting categorical exclusions, the same principles that apply to efficient, effective preparation of impact statements—making the document useful to decisionmakers by focusing concisely and clearly only on issues pertinent to the question of environmental "significance," and providing support for the ultimate determination—apply to documented categorical exclusions. The level of documentation depends largely on the type of project under study and its potential impacts.

---

20 California v. Norton, 311 F.3d 1162, 1176 (9th Cir. 2002).

Notes

_____

_____

_____

_____

_____

_____

_____

_____

_____

_____

_____

_____

_____

_____

_____

_____

_____

_____

_____

_____

Appendix

FTA Sample Letter of Invitation

U.S. Department of Transportation
Federal Transit Administration

[Insert Date]

[Insert Agency Representative]
[Insert Agency Name and Address]

Re: Invitation to Participate in the Environmental Review Process for [Insert Project Name]

Dear [Agency Representative]:

The Federal Transit Administration (FTA), in cooperation with [Insert Sponsoring Transit Agency,] is initiating the preparation of an environmental impact statement for the proposed [Insert Project Name]. The proposed project is [briefly describe action] in [describe project location]. The purpose of the project, as currently defined, is to [insert preliminary statement of the project's purpose and need]. The enclosed scoping information packet provides more details. A preliminary coordination plan and schedule [if available] are also enclosed.

Section 6002 of the Safe, Accountable, Flexible, Efficient Transportation Equity Act: A Legacy for Users (SAFETEA-LU) establishes an enhanced environmental review process for certain FTA projects, increasing the transparency of the process as well as opportunities for participation. The requirements of Section 6002 apply to the project that is the subject of this memorandum. As part of the environmental review process for this project, the lead agencies must identify, as early as practicable, any other Federal and non-Federal agencies that may have an interest in the project and invite such agencies to become participating agencies in the environmental review process.[21] Your agency has been identified preliminarily as one that may have an interest in this project, because [give reasons, such as adverse impacts, resources affected, etc., why agency may be interested]; accordingly, you are being extended this invitation to become actively involved as a participating agency in the environmental review process for the project.

---

21 Designation as a "participating agency" does not imply that the participating agency supports the proposed project or has any jurisdiction over or special expertise concerning the proposed project or its potential impacts. A "participating agency" differs from a "cooperating agency," which is defined in regulations implementing the National Environmental Policy Act as "any Federal agency other than a lead agency which has jurisdiction by law or special expertise with respect to any environmental impact involved in a proposal (or a reasonable alternative) for legislation or other major Federal action significantly affecting the quality of the human environment" (40 C.F.R. § 1508.5).

As a participating agency, you will be afforded the opportunity, together with the public, to be involved in defining the purpose of and need for the project as well as in determining the range of alternatives to be considered. In addition, you will be asked to:

- Provide input on the impact assessment methodologies and level of detail in your agency's area of expertise.
- Participate in coordination meetings, conference calls, and joint field reviews, as appropriate.
- Review and comment on sections of the pre-draft or pre-final environmental document to communicate any concerns of your agency on the adequacy of the document, the alternatives considered, and the anticipated impacts and mitigation.

Your agency does not have to accept this invitation. If, however, your agency is a Federal agency and you elect not to become a participating agency, you must decline this invitation in writing, indicating that your agency has no jurisdiction or authority with respect to the project, no expertise or information relevant to the project, and does not intend to submit comments on the project. The declination may be transmitted electronically to [insert e-mail address]; please include the title of the official responding. In order to give Federal agencies adequate opportunity to weigh the relevance of their participation in this environmental review process, written responses to this invitation are not due until after the close of the scoping process, now scheduled to conclude [insert date]. Written responses from Federal agencies declining designation as participating agencies should be transmitted to this office not later than [insert date]. You may use the attached Participating Agency Designation Form to accept or decline this invitation.

Additional information will be forthcoming during the public scoping process, notification of which will be provided in the near future. If you have questions regarding this invitation, please contact [insert name and telephone number].

Sincerely,

[Insert FTA Regional Planning Director]

Attachments: Participating Agency Designation Form
               Scoping Information Packet
               Draft Coordination Plan
               Draft Schedule (not included here)

cc: [Sponsoring Transit Agency]

[INSERT PROJECT NAME]
PARTICIPATING AGENCY DESIGNATION FORM

☐   Yes – _____ [Insert non-Federal Agency Name] wishes to be designated as a participating agency for the proposed [Insert Project Name].

☐   No – _____ [Insert non-Federal Agency Name] does not wish to be designated as a participating agency for the proposed [Insert Project Name].

☐   No – _____ [Insert Federal Agency Name] does not wish to be designated as a participating agency for the proposed [Insert Project Name] because:

        ☐   Federal agency has no jurisdiction or authority with respect to the project

        ☐   Federal agency has no expertise or information relevant to the project

        ☐   Federal agency does not intend to submit comments on the project*

_____ (Sign – Authorized Representative)

_____ (Print)

_____ (Title)

_____ (Date)

Please return by [insert date] to:

Address: [insert address]

Fax: [insert fax number]

Please note that if a Federal agency does not state its position in these terms, it should be treated as a participating agency.

SCOPING INFORMATION PACKET

DEPARTMENT OF TRANSPORTATION
Federal Transit Administration
Preparation of an Environmental Impact Statement on East-West Corridor
Transit Improvements in Metropolitan Miami, Florida

AGENCY: Federal Transit Administration (FTA), Department of Transportation.
ACTION: Notice of intent to prepare an environmental impact statement.
SUMMARY: The Federal Transit Administration and Miami-Dade Transit (MDT) are planning to prepare an environmental impact statement (EIS) for a proposed 10-mile extension of Metrorail from the Miami Intermodal Center at Miami International Airport west to Florida International University. The EIS will be prepared in accordance with regulations implementing the National Environmental Policy Act (NEPA), as well as provisions of the recently enacted Safe, Accountable, Flexible, Efficient Transportation Equity Act: A Legacy for Users (SAFETEA-LU). The purpose of this Notice of Intent (NOI) is to alert interested parties regarding the plan to prepare the EIS, to provide information on the nature of the proposed transit project, to invite participation in the EIS process, including comments on the scope of the EIS proposed in this notice, and to announce that public scoping meetings will be conducted.
DATES: Written comments on the scope of the EIS should be sent to Ms. Maria C. Batista, MDT Project Manager, by [insert date] that is at least two weeks after final scoping meeting and at least 30 days after publication of the NOI, whichever is later]. Public scoping meetings will be held on [insert date(s)] at [insert time(s)] at locations indicated under **ADDRESSES** below. An interagency scoping meeting will be scheduled after agencies with an interest in the proposed project have been identified.
ADDRESSES: Written comments on the scope of the EIS should be sent to Ms. Maria C. Batista, Project Manager, Miami-Dade Transit, 111 NW First Street, Suite 910, Miami, FL 33128-1970. Comments may also be offered at the public scoping meetings. The addresses for the public scoping meetings are as follow:

[Address for Meeting 1]
[Address for Meeting 2]

These locations are accessible to persons with disabilities. If translation signing services or other special accommodations are needed, please contact Project Manager Maria C. Batista, at [phone number] at least 48 hours before the meeting. A scoping information packet is available on the MDT Web site at:
http://www.miamidade.gov/transit/corridor/ew_corridor/scoping.pdf
or by calling the project manager, Ms. Maria C. Batista, at [phone number]. Copies will also be available at the scoping meetings.

FOR FURTHER INFORMATION CONTACT: Mr. Tony Dittmeier, Transportation Program Specialist, Federal Transit Administration, Atlanta Regional Office at [phone number].

SUPPLEMENTARY INFORMATION:

The Proposed Project: Miami-Dade Transit's proposed 10.1 mile elevated extension of Metrorail is intended to serve the East-West Corridor in an area bounded generally by NW 25th Street on the north, SW 8th Street on the south, the Homestead Extension of Florida's Turnpike (SR 821) on the west, and NW 37th Avenue to the east. The area extends approximately 1.5 miles north and south of the Dolphin Expressway (SR 836). The project area includes portions of the Cities of Miami, Sweetwater, and Doral, as well as areas within unincorporated Dade County. The proposed project would serve the airport, which is the largest trip generator in the region, as well as portions of the City of Miami along the Dolphin Expressway, the City of Sweetwater, the City of Doral, and Florida International University. Stations are proposed at the NW 57th Avenue/Blue Lagoon, NW 72nd Ave/Palmetto Expressway, NW 87th Avenue, NW 97th Avenue, NW 107th Avenue, and Florida International University.

Purposes of and Need for the Proposed Project: Recent studies of the corridor to be served by the proposed project revealed the need for transportation improvements, including a wider range of mobility options to meet increasing travel demand within and through the corridor. The project area currently has more than 195,000 residents in 68,000 households and more than 180,000 jobs. Official growth forecasts indicate that this trend will continue with population increasing by 44,000 (23 percent) by the year 2030 and jobs increasing by 60,000 (33 percent). At the present time the roadway network in the corridor is heavily congested; many segments have substantially high accident rates and unreliable travel conditions and times. Moreover, there will be little or no capacity to further expand the roadway network once the planned expansion of the Dolphin Expressway is completed.

The Miami-Dade Metropolitan Planning Organization's (MDMPO's) financially constrained 2030 Long-Range Transportation Plan, approved by its Governing Board in December 2005, and the People's Transportation Plan presented in a 2004 referendum have designated the East-West Corridor as a priority corridor for extension of Metrorail service. In November 2004, the voters of Miami-Dade County approved the People's Transportation Plan and a one-half percent sales tax increase to fund the plan. The People's Transportation Plan includes extension of Metrorail service from the Miami Intermodal Center to Florida International University.

Alternatives: The proposed project is substantially identical to a locally preferred alternative that was selected by MDT and MDMPO at the conclusion of a Major Investment Study (MIS) conducted in 2003. The MIS is available on the MDT Web site at http://www.miamidade.gov/transit/corridor/ew_corridor/MIS.pdf. Several land use and development changes that have occurred since that time prompt the need for some minor refinements to the alignment and station location options. These refinements, which are being developed in consultation with state and local agencies and the surrounding community, will be explored in the context of the EIS. The intent of the refinements is to stay generally within the original alignment while seeking to enhance ridership potential, reduce costs where feasible, and avoid, minimize, and mitigate adverse environmental impacts.

Other alternatives currently under consideration include a future no-build alternative, which contemplates roadway and transit facility and service improvements (other than the proposed project) planned for and programmed to be implemented by the year 2030. The future no-build alternative includes (1) extension of the Stage 1 Metrorail line from the existing Earlington Heights station to a new station at the Miami Intermodal Center, (2) a fixed guideway people-mover system linking the Miami Intermodal Center and the Miami International Airport, (3) an increase in Tri-Rail service frequencies to 20-minute headways during peak periods between Miami International Airport and Mangonia Park Station in Palm Beach County, and (4) continuing to comply with existing MDT policies regarding bus service and bus headways as demand in the corridor increases into the future. The future no-build alternative serves as the NEPA baseline against which environmental effects of other alternatives, including the proposed project, will be measured.

A third alternative, labeled the Transportation Systems Management alternative, is designed to provide low cost, operationally-oriented improvements to address the project's purpose and need as much as possible without a major transit investment. This alternative, which serves as the New Starts baseline against which the cost-effectiveness of the proposed project will be measured, includes, in addition to improvements identified in the no-build alternative, (1) express, limited-stop bus service along the Dolphin Expressway, (2) enhanced bus service on major east-west arterials, (3) park-and-ride facilities at the same locations as the proposed project, sized to meet anticipated demand, and (4) enhanced bus stations at the same locations as the proposed project's stations.

The EIS Process and the Role of Participating Agencies and the Public: The purpose of the EIS process is to explore in a public setting potentially significant effects of implementing the proposed action and alternatives on the physical, human, and natural environment. Areas of investigation include but are not limited to: land use, development potential, land acquisition and displacements, historic resources, visual and aesthetic qualities, air quality, noise and vibration, energy use, safety and security, and ecosystems, including threatened and endangered species. Measures to avoid, minimize, or mitigate any significant adverse impacts will be identified. Regulations implementing NEPA, as well as provisions of the recently enacted Safe, Accountable, Flexible, Efficient Transportation Equity Act: A Legacy for Users (SAFETEA-LU), call for public involvement in the EIS process. Section 6002 of SAFETEA-LU requires that FTA and MDT do the following: (1) extend an invitation to other Federal and non-Federal agencies and Indian tribes that may have an interest in the proposed project to become "participating agencies," (2) provide an opportunity for involvement by participating agencies and the public in helping to define the purpose and need for a proposed project, as well as the range of alternatives for consideration in the impact statement, and (3) establish a plan for coordinating public and agency participation in and comment on the environmental review process. An invitation to become a participating agency, with the scoping information packet appended, will be extended to other Federal and non-Federal agencies and Indian tribes that may have an interest in the proposed project. It is possible that we may not be able to identify all Federal and non-Federal agencies and Indian tribes that may have such an interest. Any Federal or non-Federal agency or Indian tribe interested in the proposed project that does not receive an invitation to become a participating agency should notify at the earliest opportunity the Project Manager identified above under **ADDRESSES**.

A comprehensive public involvement program has been developed and a public and agency involvement Coordination Plan will be created. The program includes a project Web site (http://www.miamidade.gov/transit/corridor/ew_corridor/); outreach to local and county officials and community and civic groups; a public scoping process to define the issues of concern among all parties interested in the project; establishment of a community advisory committee and organizing periodic meetings with that committee; a public hearing on release of the draft environmental impact statement (DEIS); establishment of walk-in project offices in the corridor; and development and distribution of project newsletters.

The purposes of and need for the proposed project have been preliminarily identified in this notice. We invite the public and participating agencies to consider the preliminary statement of purposes of and need for the proposed project, as well as the alternatives proposed for consideration. Suggestions for modifications to the statement of purposes of and need for the proposed project and any other alternatives that meet the purposes of and need for the proposed project are welcomed and will be given serious consideration. Comments on potentially significant environmental impacts that may be associated with the proposed project and alternatives are also welcomed. There will be additional opportunities to participate in the scoping process at the public meetings announced in this notice.

Miami-Dade Transit is seeking New Starts funding for the proposed project under 49 U.S.C. 5309 and will therefore be subject to New Starts regulations (49 CFR Part 611). The New Starts regulation requires the submission of specific information in support of a request to initiate preliminary engineering, and this information is normally developed in conjunction with the NEPA process. Pertinent New Starts evaluation criteria will be included in the final environmental impact statement.

In accordance with 23 CFR 771.105(a) and 771.133, FTA will comply with all Federal environmental laws, regulations, and executive orders applicable to the proposed project during the environmental review process to the maximum extent practicable. These requirements include, but are not limited to, the regulations of the Council on Environmental Quality and FTA implementing NEPA (40 CFR parts 1500-1508, and 23 CFR Part 771), the project-level air quality conformity regulation of the U.S. Environmental Protection Agency (EPA) (40 CFR part 93), the Section 404(b)(1) guidelines of EPA (40 CFR part 230), the regulation implementing Section 106 of the National Historic Preservation Act (36 CFR Part 800), the regulation implementing section 7 of the Endangered Species Act (50 CFR part 402), Section 4(f) of the Department of Transportation Act (23 CFR 771.135), and Executive Orders 12898 on environmental justice, 11988 on floodplain management, and 11990 on wetlands.
Issued On: [date signed].
Ms. Yvette G. Taylor
Regional Administrator, FTA Region 4

DRAFT COORDINATION PLAN

Note: This is a "bare-bones" sample coordination plan that anticipates involvement of participating agencies and the public in determining the purpose and need for a project as well as the range of alternatives to be considered in the context of the scoping process. If the plan is going to include a schedule, certain factors enumerated in 23 U.S.C. § 139(g)(1)(B)(ii) must be considered; additionally, the schedule must be consistent with any other relevant time periods established under Federal law.

[Project Identifier]

Section 6002 of the Safe, Accountable, Flexible, Efficient Transportation Equity Act: A Legacy for Users (SAFETEA-LU) created a new Section 139 of Title 23 of the U.S.C. mandating, among other requirements, that the lead agency must establish a plan for coordinating public and agency participation in and comment on the environmental review process for a project or category of projects. As part of the coordination plan, and after consulting with each participating agency and with the State in which the project is located or the project sponsor, the lead agency may establish a schedule for completion of the environmental review process for the project. This coordination plan, which does not include a schedule, is being established for the above-named project.

Sequential Opportunities for Participating Agency and Public Involvement

Notice of intent: Comments on the Notice of Intent [if published, identify by volume/number/Federal Register page number/year] and information contained in the notice are invited. The comment due date is [insert date].

Scoping: The process for determining the scope of issues to be addressed in the impact statement and for identifying significant issues related to the project will be conducted as follows:

Draft environmental impact statement: A Federal Register notice will announce the availability for comment of the draft environmental impact statement and fix the commenting period. The announcement will also be published in a local newspaper of general circulation.

Public hearing: A public hearing will be held during the public review/circulation period for the draft environmental impact statement. Notice of the public hearing will be published in a local newspaper of general circulation and by other available means.

Other opportunities: As appropriate.

Opportunity for Additional Involvement by Participating Agencies

Methodologies: The lead agency, in collaboration with participating agencies at appropriate times during the study process, must determine the methodologies to be used and the level of detail required in the analysis of each alternative for a project. Notice to participating agencies of such collaborative opportunities will be provided by the lead agency.

Other Key Points in the Environmental Process

In addition to opportunities for public and participating agency involvement in the environmental process identified above, other key points in that process include:

Final environmental impact statement: Issued through a notice of availability published in the Federal Register by the U.S. Environmental Protection Agency and through publication in a local newspaper of general circulation.

Record of decision: The record of decision concludes the environmental process and will normally be provided to anyone who received a copy of the final environmental impact statement.

This coordination plan will be made available to participating agencies and to the public upon request.

Lead Agency Contact: [insert contact]

Notes

Index

Keys to Efficient Development
of Useful Environmental Documents

Federal Transit Administration
1200 New Jersey Ave. SE
4th & 5th Floors, East Building
Washington, DC 20590

Office of Communications and Congressional Affairs (202) 366-4043

 U.S. Department of Transportation

FTA-MA-26-1023-2007.1